James John, the founder of Love, Appreciate, Forgive (LAF), has written his first children's book with his beautiful family. *How to Love Myself and Others* introduces young children how to truly love themselves every day. Once they learn how to fill themselves up with self-love, it shows them how to give love to others no matter what people look like or where they come from. This book offers the opportunity for parents and children to talk about values that are the foundation of a truly happy life.

Remembering we all come from one love, let's go back there together.

Balboa Press books may be ordered through booksellers or by contacting:

Balboa Press
A Division of Hay House
1663 Liberty Drive
Bloomington, IN 47403
www.balboapress.com
1 (877) 407-4847

www.livinglaf.com

ISBN: 978-1-5043-2700-8 (sc)
ISBN: 978-1-5043-2701-5 (e)

Print information available on the last page.

Balboa Press rev. date: 03/03/2015

BALBOA
PRESS
A DIVISION OF HAY HOUSE

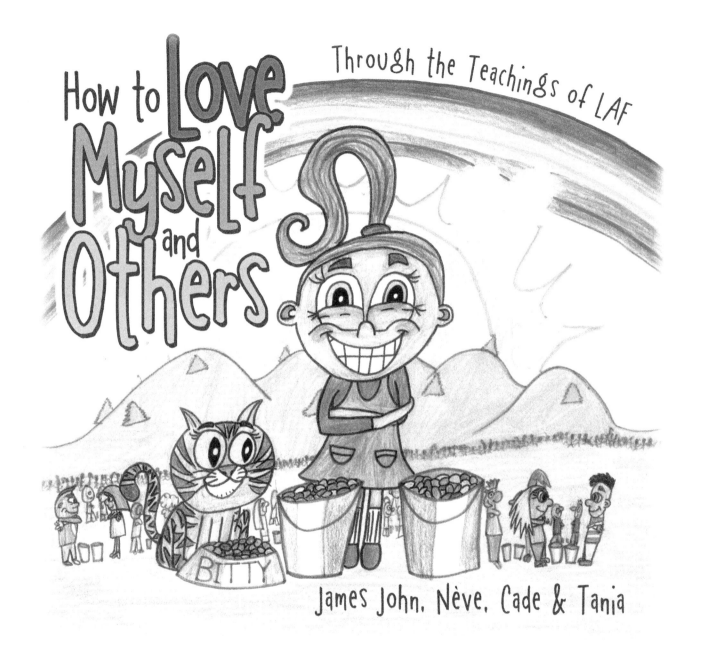

How to Love Myself and Others

Through the Teachings of LAF

James John, Nève, Cade & Tania

BITTY

illustrated by Cade, age 11

A very special thank you to:
Rose S, Vittoria B, Sharon S, Jennifer C, Khris M, Adele P, Sandee T and Cathy L

There are so many beautiful things to love in this world like our parents, friends and animals.

3

ABCDEFGHIJKLMNOPQRSTUVW
XYZ
5x1=5
5x2=10
5x3=15
Pod
Peas
1
5
2
3
4
5
D

There are also things that happen in our lives
that make us feel bad about ourselves and
we forget how special we really are.

But sometimes we forget to love the most important person of us all; ourselves.

Having that special love for yourself means that you are proud of the person you have become. You like being yourself and that makes you feel joyful and happy. It also helps you to love others.

When you have self love, people can see the beauty in you and they would want to love you and become your friend even more.

It does not matter what you look like; tall or short, skinny or fluffy. It doesn't matter the color of your skin and hair, or being in a wheel chair.

We all came from the same place.

We all came from Love.

Now, how do we love ourselves?

It's easy!

You fill yourself up with love just like you would
fill up a bucketful of colorful jelly beans.

When looking at yourself in the mirror you can say things like, "I love you" and "You are beautiful" or "You are handsome". You can even give yourself a big bear hug. Let's do that now.

If someone hurts your feelings or calls you names, they are wrong. They never filled themselves up with love before so they can't see the beauty within you.

So, how do we love others?

You share it.

Once you fill yourself up with all of that love, you begin to overflow, just like a bucket would overflow with those colorful jelly beans. So give some away!

JELLYBEANS

23

Just imagine how much love you can give to all of your family, friends and animals because you are always over-flowing with so much love.

You can even give some to the kid who hurt your feelings because they never filled themselves up with love before. Isn't that a good idea?

So always remember to hug yourself and
fill up with lots of love every single day.
So you can have self-love, be happy and
help others to fill up with love too.

The LAF prayer

I Love myself and everything
I Appreciate myself and everything
I Forgive myself and everything
I LAF

The End

"The greatest gift we can give our children is to show them how to live, not telling them."

-James John

CPSIA information can be obtained
at www.ICGtesting.com
Printed in the USA
LVOW05s1347070317
526333LV00001B/1/P